CW00684747

Tiny
essentials of
writing for
fundraising

by George Smith

Published by
The White Lion Press Limited
Kermarquer
56310 Melrand
France

ISBN 0-9518971-6-0

First printed 2003

British Library Cataloguing-in-Publication Data.
A catalogue record for this book is available from the British Library.

Model: Elisa Merlo
Photograpy by Adrian Taylor
Design and print production by *e*m associates
Printed and bound in the United Kingdom by
The Baskerville Press, Salisbury

Contents

The author

George Smith wrote his first fundraising ad as long ago as 1962 – for Oxfam. In his late twenties he was appointed European coordinator for a major-league American advertising agency and, by way of contrast, was elected as a councillor in an inner-London borough. He formed the celebrated Smith Bundy agency in 1973 and served as chief executive for 20 years. Additionally he was chief executive of the International Fund Raising Group, now the Resource Alliance, between 1987 and 1993 and a director of Burnett Associates from 1983 to 1999. He became chairman of Britain's Institute of Direct Marketing in 1997 and is an honorary fellow both of the IDM and the Institute of Fundraising.

Preface

Much of the content of this book derives from the much longer *Asking Properly* published in 1996. I have updated that content and bolted on a number of new observations. But my general message remains the same – that charities and their suppliers should simply learn to write better so that they can raise more money.

It's something I feel even more strongly about as the years pass and as fundraising performance declines (it does, you know).

So, if you sense anger throbbing away behind these paragraphs, forgive me. And I do hope that this modest manual helps you think better about using words to persuade people to give.

George Smith
November 2003

Author's note

My publishers have been kind enough not to change too many of the words with which I supplied them. It's a very British book, I know, and probably a slightly eccentric one these days. But I did find that its content played well when I built a seminar around it a few years back. I remember doing it throughout Europe and in venues like Nairobi, Atlanta and Toronto. I don't recall too many furrowed brows and I do remember the flattering verdict of 'refreshing' on lots of evaluation forms. I was always happy with that, for all I ever wanted to do was to *provoke* people to think about the words they use.

In that spirit, I offer this little book. Please forgive any occasional parochialism. We still use the word 'charity' in the UK to cover most kinds of nonprofit or voluntary organisation and you will also find other examples of Brit-speak. But I don't think they should sap the message. I hope not anyway.

GS

Too many words, too little meaning

We live in a verbally jaded world.

That's probably a bad start to a book like this. In fact, stick that first sentence in front of almost any fundraiser and expect confusion, anxiety, suspicion and emerging hostility.

'Verbally'? Isn't that something to do with talking?

'Jaded'? Isn't that something to do with a colour? Or a precious stone, or something? Wasn't that large girl on *Big Brother* called Jade?

I'll try again. We live in a world where words are increasingly without meaning. Where the cliché rules. Where the power of words to explain, to communicate and to convince is currently in abeyance.

I just got posh again. So let me say it loud and plain – this is the Age of Bullshit. We all know it. We all let it wash over us. We don't quite believe or disbelieve any more. We hear things vaguely. We read things vaguely. So, the use of language to explain and clarify has declined. A vacuum has been created and it has been partially filled with a new phenomenon.

For we live in the first age of Verbal Predictability. For the very first time in recorded history *you know what someone is going to say before they say it.*

So let me say it loud and plain – this is the Age of Bullshit.

This strange new truth already has its own rituals. How did we ever get used to a form of words like 'Mr Blair is expected to say today'. Or the worldwide convention of two television presenters sitting behind a desk reading alternate paragraphs off a teleprompter. Or the reporter walking towards the camera waving his arms to suggest *gravitas*. Or the obscure celebrity sitting on a chat-show sofa telling us that his most recent show/film/record/interview was the best thing he's ever done. For these strange new customs – they are no more than 10 years old – are indeed worldwide. And again they serve to diminish meaning or content – the audience watches with one eye closed, the brain stalled, the capacity to judge or even react stifled.

The world is now governed by the media. Which means that it is governed by the teleprompter. And, if you have ever had to read something off a teleprompter, you'll know what a stultifying and dehumanising process it is. You begin to sound like everyone else. You have lost your individual voice.

And another thing...

This is therefore the age of prolixity – of excess words filling the space afforded by the means of expressing those words – the media again. Hundreds of radio and television channels have to be filled with something and are filled with dross – the ramblings of the presenter, the opinions of the phone-in callers and latterly the recitations of the e-mailers. You would not want to be stuck in a lift with any of these people but there they are in your house day or night.

And what are people communicating over mobile phones that could not have been thus communicated 15 years ago? Gibberish usually. How much content is there in the average office e-mail? Bugger all. It's words filling space again, I fear.

Everyone feels the need to say more than is necessary. A cornflake packet now carries enough words for a short story. A weather forecast can fill its five minutes by telling you about today's weather as well as tomorrow's. Three commentators will discuss an endlessly replayed goal. So many words, so little meaning, so little attention!

And it's irritating too. My favourite current example is the cinema, now subject to the new demands of 'branding'. I enter the Odeon while strobe lights scan the corridors telling me that I am in the Odeon. I am subjected to ads by Kodak and Dolby who want me to know that they play a part in proceedings. And, yes, I am subjected to a clip from the Odeon chain telling me that they show films.

I knew this already. But you want to scream at the screen. *'I know you show films. It's why I'm sitting here. Sod you, Odeon.'*

All these new and malign things define the world in which the fundraiser tries to do his or her job. Let me repeat the sixth word I used: jaded. That's how people are these days. They've heard everything several times over and you are going to have to express yourself remarkably well to catch their attention and persuade them to give you money.

This little book is dedicated to trying harder with words in the belief that raising money to do good is still an honourable occupation, no matter how shabby and weary its tradecraft has become.

Think before you start

See yourself as others see you.

You call it an appeal, a recruitment mailing, a household delivery package, a supporters update.

They call it a begging letter. Junk mail these days always includes begging letters.

So they don't like you. That's before they listen to a word you've said. They've decoded what you've said on the envelope, be it ever so involving, and decided that it's a begging letter. You are already in the waste-bin together with the double-glazing flier and that day's credit card invitation pack.

The hardest truth about fundraising direct mail is less the pitiful number who ever respond but the rising majority who never even considered responding. They never ever noticed what you had to say. It is now probably true that most fundraising direct mail is thrown away unopened at a unit cost of upwards of 50p.

For, how else can you explain recruitment mailings where more than 99 people in a hundred fail to respond? Or 'supporter' mailings where 90 'supporters' in a hundred fail to respond? These are now familiar response statistics and they are about a third of what a charity might have expected 10 or 15 years ago. Too much competitive activity? Certainly. Customer indifference? Most likely. Customer irritation? Very much so.

All the more reason for trying to think better about what we're trying to say.

Who the hell do you think you are?

You are asking someone for money. This is something you'll not have done in physical terms for a long time. You probably asked your parents for money at some stage, you may have tapped a friend when in distress and, if you are old enough, you may remember the days when you had to ask banks and building societies for financial help rather than merely accept their regularly-offered blandishments.

You may even have shaken a diffident collecting tin at strangers in the hope of stray coins. But, unless you personally work for a face-to-face fundraising outfit, you certainly haven't eyeballed those strangers and asked for £15. And this is what you are doing when you write that appeal letter. A certain humility is called for before you start. And a lot of self-awareness.

Ask yourself – mentally at least – three questions.

1. Why am I sending this letter?

2. Why, precisely, do I need money right now?

3. What am I going to do with it when I get it?

This may sound primitive but the questions still need an answer. And you need to answer objectively. Most fundraisers' answer to the first question would probably be 'Because it's the April appeal', or some such. Not good enough; that's a domestic routine being reported, not a need.

The most successful appeal will always report urgent need; you need to construct that need with integrity and flourish.

Similarly with the second question. The charity probably has millions of pounds in the bank when it asks for your £15, so what's the problem? The most successful appeal will always report urgent need; you need to construct that need with integrity and flourish.

The third question is always more difficult. Charities prefer general funding to earmarked or project-specific funding – their hands are left free to spend where the need is greatest. But we all know that an emergency appeal will out-perform a general appeal and that a single subject will do better than a general message. A greater credence attaches to a specific request. Again, think of it as a physical one-to-one task. Would you have asked your dad for £50 without saying how you would be spending it? Explaining how money is to be used is surely simple courtesy.

Explaining how money is to be used is surely simple courtesy.

Some new – and awkward – truths

So far the homilies have been eternal, chunks of sheer common sense that should always inform the process of asking for money. But things change and there are some recent changes that make the process even harder.

Take the concept of 'supporters'. They used to be the first generation of people who had rallied to a cause, the committee members, the regional and local workers, the good folk who did the house-to-house collections or, indeed, shook those collecting tins. They are still around but take a closer look – they are old, these supporters, for they have probably been involved now for decades.

Statistically, the majority of a charity's 'supporters' are now different from the traditional kind. For they have been *recruited* – by mail, by phone, by being stopped in the street. Indeed you have probably paid £50 (or much more) to recruit each of them and persuaded yourself that this is a sound investment. But it is a totally different relationship. Formerly supporters initiated the relationship. Now the charity initiates the relationship. It is the difference between a conscript army and an army of volunteers and it would be daft if we did not acknowledge the importance of this. There is likely to be less affection and admiration involved and a greater suspicion. For the relationship is rooted in a financial transaction and nothing more elevated; you asked and they said yes.

So they don't 'belong' in the sense that their predecessors did. It could be that they don't actually much like you. It is probably true that they know little about you. It is certainly a statistical fact that they support at least two other charities besides you. And it is an emerging fact that they will not be with you for decades to come. If they were recruited by face-to-face marketing (as over a million new donors have been in the last few years), they will probably not be with you in three years time.

Pretending that this new kind of relationship is akin to the previous one is a sentimental and dangerous untruth. And to call these donors 'supporters' is to use the word very loosely. They are nice people who once gave you money and who may still, in response to your vigorous advocacy of the direct debit, give you money on a regular basis. But you should never patronise them or presume on the depth of their zeal for your work. Appeal mailings to 'supporters' raise a fraction of what they used to in percentage terms, a decline explained by the new shallowness of the relationship. But, like all negative observations, it offers a positive opportunity.

As does the second recent addendum to the old rules. It's a simple statement but one that should give pause to anyone writing an appeal letter.

It is the difference between a conscript army and an army of volunteers...

It's this. *No one writes personal letters any more.*

Think about it. When is the last time a friend wrote you a letter? Put aside the functional uses of the form – the thank-you notes, the announcements and invitations, the complaints and enquiries. When is the last time you received (or wrote) a letter containing news, observation, thoughts, stories, descriptions, aspirations or gossip?

When is the last time you saw – or even heard of – a love letter?

The tradition of personal expression in letter form, a tradition that had graced literature and culture for hundreds of years, died very suddenly in the 1990s. We now phone, text, or e-mail and the quality of the average utterance via these media tells its own story. We have become brutishly inelegant in our messages to each other, abbreviating, crudifying, simplifying. The letter still exists but only as a mass-produced component of a direct mail pack. Even the message on the holiday postcard is probably now e-mailed.

So, I suggest your heart would soar if – once in a while – you received a letter written in decent English which said unexpected things in elegant ways, which moved you and stirred your emotions, which angered you or made you proud, a letter which you wanted to read from beginning to end, a letter apparently written by one individual to another individual. For you never see these letters any more.

This is not a plea for a revival of the epistolary tradition. I am just suggesting that charities could fill this recently created gap in all our lives. They are, after all, trying to communicate important things to intelligent people. Why not do it properly and use the full power of the English language?

Say what you mean.

Right at the start I made the point – if it needed making – that we live in a world where words are increasingly without meaning, where clichés rule, where obfuscation (look it up!) has become a minor art form.

I attended a senior management meeting with a big-league charity recently. This was the agenda.

- Core purpose

- Values
- Differentiator
- Essence
- Mission
- Vision
- Key messages
- Outcomes

Why not do it properly and use the full power of the English language?

Yes, it was that kind of navel-gazing meeting – you have probably attended one or two yourself. Within half an hour, we were talking about 'ring-fencing the stakeholders'. It was in many ways a sad session for these were good and intelligent people. But, in deference to the nature of the occasion, an alien vocabulary had to be used, the language of management consultants. It served the meeting badly, concealing real problems and real opportunities under a blanket of comfortable second-hand verbiage. It actually makes for cynicism – participants were sniggering over the 'ring-fencing the stakeholders' construct at the first coffee break (not that anyone was going to be rude about it out loud).

And the saddest thing of all? Not one of this charity's donors, whatever their age, whatever their background, whatever their education, would have understood what the hell these highly-paid people were doing. Only as a veteran of such proceedings did I have an inkling of what we were talking about.

The Age of Bullshit, then. An age where gibberish and jargon are deployed to confuse the audience and enable the authors to posture as authoritative. An age where the following sentence can solemnly make its way into print.

High-quality learning environments are a necessary precondition for facilitation and enhancement of the ongoing learning process.

Which mighty statement can be expressed as,

Children need good schools if they are to learn properly.

But then it was barely worth saying anyway.

An age where gibberish and jargon are deployed to confuse the audience and enable the authors to posture as authoritative.

What really matters creatively

There are five things that should be in the back of your mind every time you prepare a piece of fundraising communication.

1. Who am I talking to?

2. What precisely am I asking them to do?

3. Why?

4. Have I made the message sound important – or evocative, passionate, crucial, urgent…? Select your own epithets, but you'll need most of them

5. Have I done something that has never quite been done before?

Of these, only the fifth is really a luxury. The rest are fundamental demands on your communication, though more honoured in the breach than in the observance. Which is why we need to spend a little time with them.

Who am I talking to?

You are communicating with thousands, maybe hundreds of thousands, of people who you don't know and who you will never meet.. But it's still worth trying to picture them in your mind's eye. How old are they? What gender are they? What do they eat?

Frankly, picturing your audience is no more than a creative device. Your chances of sociological accuracy are minute. But it is vital that we peel away the lazy words that we use to describe an audience and expose a real, breathing human being underneath. The average brief will give you a dull litany of categories – ABC1s, regular donors, lapsed donors, female investors, ACORN category B21, university educated, *Guardian* readers. But every one of the people with whom you are trying to communicate is an individual. Try and get a fix on that individual. You are talking to a real person not a list.

Try Mrs Jones, aged 45. She is worried about her weight and how to transport her 15-year-old daughter back from the disco on Saturday. She wants to plant those shrubs she just bought and finish that Catherine Cookson her friend lent her.

She's furious with her husband who wants to go back to Spain for the umpteenth time this summer. She couldn't be bothered to vote at the last election.

I can see her now, can't you? She's the lady over there in the cardigan from Marks and Spencer. We shall communicate better because we have drawn this entirely notional picture of her. For we would not shout at Mrs Jones. We would not seek to alarm her unduly. We would not confuse her with long words. Picturing her gives us the language we would use if we were privileged to be talking to her direct. Do you use the same words to your mum as you would use to your mates in the pub?

Give money is your puzzled answer.

Come to think of it, you could perhaps think of your mum every time you write a piece of fundraising communication. She is probably the likeliest model of the average donor you will ever meet.

What precisely am I asking them to do?

Give money is your puzzled answer. But anyone bemused by my question would be well advised to spread out a collection of charity ads and mailings on the desk. For they will often be asking for money in strange ways, ways that the potential donor will have to decode more often than you think.

Take the infamous 'survey pack', that proven gambit for securing the reader's involvement. It affects to be a genuine piece of research and, when these packs were launched a decade or so ago, it could claim to be a modest version of genuine fact-finding on the charity's behalf. At least someone used to compile some of the answers to the questions posed and summarise the result for anyone interested.

No one seems to have had a creative look at a reply form for a generation.

Innocent days! The 'survey packs' are now pure contrivance, gulling ordinary people into participation and then – and sometimes – giving. Yes, they do better than an ordinary household distribution pack but so would physical violence. We have merely evolved a faintly disreputable way of getting response, complete with free pen. It is an odd – a very odd – way to ask for money.

But there are plenty of other circuitous approaches to the art of asking. The face-to-face recruiter will offer the gnomic 'Have you got two minutes for Alzheimer's?' The plastic-wrapped appeal that arrived this morning from my local wildlife trust tells me, before anything else happens, that 50 per cent of the UK's wildlife lives in the sea. And the reply form in this mailing offers me a range of donation options via tick boxes ranging from £10 to £5,000.

Study the average charity reply form to see how we confuse the simple issue of giving by assembling the apparatus of form-filling. There are the tick boxes, there is the credit card panel, there is the GiftAid (tax recovery) paragraph, there is the Data Protection sentence, there is the address panel. No one seems to have had a creative look at a reply form for a generation.

Today's starts with that immortal affirmative declaration, only seen in direct marketing, 'YES,' it says, 'I would like to help save and protect Kent's wildlife'.

No one would ever say such a thing out loud. But then 'Have you got two minutes for Alzheimer's?' is a pretty odd thing to say as well.

Why?

Talk about your own organisation too much and you risk shrugged shoulders, even among those apparently committed supporters. So, your twenty-fifth anniversary, your change of name from the Bewildered Fund to DAZE, or the chance to scale Himalayan peaks on your behalf are merely domestic issues and nothing directly to do with need.

Every disaster appeal tells you the value of the specific. The development charities may be slightly sniffy these days about emergency appeals but they owe the size of their mailing lists to decades of floods, earthquakes, cyclones and famines. And an organisation like Greenpeace rightly sees its news coverage as the fuel for its fundraising. Issues and events are important.

But every organisation can create its own news, even though its dissemination may be restricted to its appeal programmes. Often the news may be bad – which is probably good for fundraising. Maybe the old people's home has been refused a fire certificate. Maybe the vandals smashed up the Family Centre over the weekend. Maybe a grant from a trust is coming to an end.

And no one says to their partner, 'Honey, the appeal mailings have arrived'.

Sharing such intimate little details of your organisation's work does two things. It articulates the need and dramatises it. If the old people's home needs £30,000 on fire precaution equipment, if the Family Centre needs redecorating to the tune of £20,000, if the charity is going to be short of £50,000 a year come January, then the donor is being offered a reason to give.

Sharing your tribulations and making news of them does something else. It makes you sound human. It gives you the language of one friend to another, the quiet honesty of everyday speech. And the stories themselves are no weaker for being mundane. Can't you imagine those vandalised children's toys at the Family Centre? Can't you picture the old folk who will have to be moved from their rooms? Not all need is melodramatic. Indeed, humble events can often have greater credibility.

But there should always be a brisk and colourful answer to the question 'Why should I send you money?'

It is a fair question, after all.

Have I made the message sound important?

No one starts the day with the intention of making a charity donation. And no one says to their partner, 'Honey, the appeal mailings have arrived'.

A routine charity appeal has to fight its way through torpor. It actually has a harder task than ordinary product advertising, where the advertiser can make a reasonable assumption that the reader or viewer is in weekly need of cereals, seasonal need of things for the garden and perhaps an annual need for a new car. Fundraisers cannot presume on this perceived importance. They have to create it.

News headlines, as we have already seen, often create the importance for us. Many charities have learned to provoke news stories through the media. But this still leaves most routine charity appeals devoid of 'a sense of event'.

It is a phrase I have used for years now. When I do, people tend to skitter off into the most literal directions. But I am not talking about anniversaries, birthdays, or the launch of a multi-million pound appeal. As I have said, these are of only domestic interest and are rarely evocative in themselves.

A sense of event can be purely personal. Today I

have agreed to sponsor a whale. Today I have made a contribution to the local hospice. Today I have committed myself to political prisoners in Paraguay. These are the things we want people to do and we can persuade them to do them by elevating their importance.

In producing creative work that asks for money, it is usually worth bolting into your head a melodramatic description of the reaction you are trying to evoke in your reader's mind. I offer a lurid version.

An appeal does not acquire a sense of urgency by being labelled with the wan word 'Urgent'.

Unless I give £20 to this appeal today, people will die and suffer things I have never suffered. I can stop these things happening tomorrow. I shall not miss the £20 and I know that it can achieve marvellous things in other hands. I will have done something remarkable today by sending this donation.

Too strong, too simple-minded? I wonder. You can temper these words, you can adapt them to become more appropriate to your organisation. But you should not pretend that the reader has any higher instinct than rising to the rhetorical challenge that they depict. They make the donation sound both important and distinctive.

Do not underestimate the degree to which every part of a mailing can contribute to this sense of importance. But do not delude yourself that it can be created with routine language, familiar visuals, last year's clichés. An appeal does not acquire a sense of urgency by being labelled with the wan word 'Urgent'. A message does not acquire importance by being solemnly labelled 'Important'. The constant deployment of these words has rendered them meaningless.

Have I done something that has never quite been done before?

As I said at the beginning of this section, this is a luxury item among a list of essentials. But it is an ambition still worth conjuring out of an apparently commonplace brief. So much fundraising communication is now formulaic that the merest adventure, the smallest piece of pioneering will stand out from the crowd.

'All great truths start off as blasphemies' said George Bernard Shaw. Fundraising now needs its blasphemers. For it has become a business characterised by fear and deference. Fundraisers preside where they should innovate. All wisdom is conventional, all practice derivative. 'They must know what they're doing,' says one charity of another's programme. Believe me, the respect is often misplaced.

We will always need new variants on trusted themes. I think of the YMCA campaign that stuck a pound coin on a card. I think of the WWF legacy campaign that majored on the little-known word ‘intestacy’. I think of the first charity that wrote a four-page letter and the first charity that just sent a compliments slip. I think of barmy Bob Geldof aiming to fill Wembley Stadium with 90,000 people and that unworldly bunch who thought you could make money out of comedians and call it (ugggh!) *Comic Relief*. They must all have been blasphemies in the fact of contemporary truth.

Someone will always say ‘you can’t do that’. They are almost always wrong. Novelty is not always a virtue. But innovation is a constant necessity.

It is vital that we peel away the lazy words that we use to describe an audience and expose a real, breathing human being underneath.

The art of writing

No one ever felt more keenly about the English language than George Orwell. He was an enemy of cant in any form and particularly waspish about the abuse of English by politicians, bureaucrats and those in power generally. No one has ever rivalled the glittering common sense he offers us in Politics and the English Language, an essay written as long ago as 1946. I am happy to quote from it extensively because its succinctness has never been bettered.

He offered as instruction a list of six questions that every writer should ask of himself or herself

1. What am I trying to say?
2. What words will express it?
3. What image or idiom will make it clearer?

4. Is the image fresh enough to make the effect?

5. Could I put it more shortly?

6. Have I said anything that is avoidably ugly?

A little later on, he offers an even more challenging list

1. Never use a metaphor, simile, or other figure of speech that you are used to seeing in print.

2. Never use a long word where a short one will do.

3. If it is possible to cut a word out, cut it out.

4. Never use the passive voice when you can use the active voice.

'Correct grammar and syntax are of no importance as long as one makes one's meaning clear.'

5. Never use a foreign phrase, a scientific word, or a jargon word if you can think of an everyday English equivalent.

6. Break any of these rules sooner than say anything outright barbarous.

Notoriously, Orwell was a demanding old cuss. How on earth can you avoid totally any figure of speech that you are used to seeing in print? But it is amusing to consider how he would react to the shoddy, useless, lazy language with which we are surrounded 60 years after he wrote this essay. For his verdict on modern writing has never been bettered.

Modern writing at its worst does not consist of picking out words for the sake of their meaning and inventing images to make the meaning clearer. It consists of gumming together long strips of words, which have already been set in order by someone else, and making the results presentable by sheer humbug.

As I say, this was written nearly 60 years ago and only the use of the word 'humbug' gives its age away. Otherwise it is a word-perfect judgment. *Long strips of words, which have already been set in order by someone else...* How much fundraising copy can escape that Orwellian verdict?

When you quote homilies like those of Orwell to a contemporary audience, you stand accused of would-be donnishness, of a certain pretentious posing. It is as if you were dragging hardbitten professionals back to the schoolroom, when they were forced to read hated texts and learn dumb rules about English grammar. Orwell is a dead, white author, right?

Yes and an old Etonian to boot. But he was a radical and a puritan as well. This is what he said in 1950.

Correct grammar and syntax are of no importance as long as one makes one's meaning clear.

Amen to that!

Things not to worry about...

The rules of English grammar are long-forgotten. This is what the Government's Board of Education reported when Gladstone was still Prime Minister.

There is no such thing as English grammar in the sense which used to be attached to the term.

So you can lay waste to some common grammatical myths.

Of course you can begin a sentence with 'and' – 30 of the first 31 sentences in the King James Bible do just that.

Of course you can split infinitives. Pedants have been sneering at 'to boldly go' on the *Star Trek* credits for 30-odd years. But its meaning is perfectly clear.

Of course you can end a sentence with a preposition. What are those little words for?

Grammar matters less than style, content matters more than syntax. In fundraising copy, what matters most is the power that the language gives us to convey emotion and need. The distinctions between gerunds and gerundives, or the proper uses of the adverbial clause of concession are unlikely to help.

The practice of writing

I have listed what Orwell told us about writing in general. It is now time to get closer to our own particular demands in writing fundraising copy. If it checks out with Orwell from time to time, do not be the least surprised, for it is my strongly-held belief that fundraising communication does not need its own specially fabricated language.

Use Saxon words and not Latin ones

Ninety-five per cent of words in the English language come from either Saxon or Latin roots.

The former are shorter and therefore better. Look at these familiar alternatives

Latin	*Saxon*
Information	News, facts
Indicate	Show
Immediately	Now, right away
Construct	Build, make
Discover	Find

The Saxon words have more force. If you don't believe me, try swearing with Latin-based oaths.

Use vivid words and not hackneyed ones

Sounds obvious, doesn't it? But I suggest that you challenge your next piece of fundraising copy in these terms. Start with the reply device, then look at the body copy of an ad or the text of a letter. How many times could you have used a substitute word to greater point?

Nothing need be sacred. Back in the seventies the only tax-effective charity gift in Britain was called a covenant, a four-year regular commitment by the donor which qualified for tax relief. The covenant form always loyally bore the heading 'Covenant Form'. Until we changed it – perfectly legally – to 'Tax Recovery Form'. Response accelerated immediately.

Use short sentences and vary the lengths

The full stop is there for a reason. It helps people understand what you are saying by chopping your text into bite-size pieces called sentences. Remember: nothing else matters except meaning. A sentence does not need a verb. Not at all. It need not defer to the Johnsonian tradition of the periodic sentence that ran to perhaps 200 words complete with sub-clauses and the full complement of colons and semicolons to separate the various constructs, a tradition that continued in the hands of writers such as Henry James, an author who rarely deployed 20 words when 200 could fulfil his sense of personal grandeur, a quality that some may admire but which most would resist on the basis that there are only so many hours in the day in which to read a novel.

You are a charity. People expect you to be asking for money.

Did you fall asleep during that last sentence? Good. I have made my point. A long sentence is not just damned hard work, it also provokes the language of pomposity and self-regard. Short sentences are more appropriate to fundraising. Like this. But not always. Boredom sets in. Truly it does. Honestly. See what I mean?

And I play these games because the short and verb-free sentence has become just a little bit of a cliché in its own right. Sentence length should be varied. It helps the reader understand what you are trying to say. That's all.

Use short paragraphs and vary the lengths

A similar but separate point. You can create a powerful paragraph out of just one sentence. But if every paragraph – or succeeding paragraphs – is so leanly constructed, then the power is lost and the ghost of professional technique begins to haunt your message.

Avoid the temptation to write snappy little paragraphs like these.

They can work. But not always.

In fact, they can be boring.

And I hope the paragraphs above prove the point. The paragraph I am writing now is, ironically, much easier for you to read. It is also more courteous, for short sentences in short paragraphs have a habit of sounding like slogans.

Get to the point!

You are a charity. People expect you to be asking for money. So, do not delay the primary reason for communicating. Do not feel that you have to lead up to your vulgar request via 200 words of self-justification, for nothing is more tiresome than an over-long preamble to a predictable request. Would a tax demand be more acceptable if it offered a couple of paragraphs about the history of the Inland Revenue, or an update on the trade deficit?

Get real!

There is a certain kind of letter that only exists as an appeals letter. It has two or four pages, it has a

PS and, quite often, a PPS. It may have photographs interspersed in the text and it will certainly make full play with the available type styles. It will make an important point by slipping into italics *so that your eye is directed to the sentence in question.* It will make a very important point by using a bold face **so that its importance is hammered home**. Or it will underline something so that you fully understand what is being said. Combinations of two or three of these typographic variants are not unknown.

No real person ever sent you a letter like this. This is why hardly anyone ever reads them. They reflect thoughtless tradecraft, born of deference to an old-fashioned model of mail order writing and not to fundraising messages. Again, think of your communication in physical terms. Which moves you most – the dignity of quiet persuasion, or a set of screeching slogans?

Use active verbs and not passive ones

A direct echo of Orwell, I know, but charities do have a habit of slipping into the passive voice – I suspect because they think it makes them sound somehow more corporate. But, as the excellent Plain English Campaign points out (www.plainenglish.co.uk, seeing as you ask) the use of the passive voice with its reversal of subject and object can be very confusing and tiresome. And it certainly smacks of bureaucracy where 'Your letter has been received' will always be preferred to 'We have received your letter'.

Charities need the vigour of the active voice. Compare and contrast,

Tents will be sent to Kurdistan as a matter of urgency.

with

We must send those tents to Kurdistan urgently.

Relate the story to the reader

It is possible more often than you might think. And it is always worth trying if only because many people's donations are subliminal thank-offerings. They look at the pictures of hungry children and reflect on their own healthy brood. They read about mistreatment of animals while their own much-loved dog sits at their feet. They grieve over medical conditions which they will never experience.

'Give to others less fortunate than yourselves' is one of the very oldest fundraising mantra but it is a sound one still. You have to be a little more linguistically subtle, of course, these days and you should always avoid the outright mawkishness that can creep in. A sentence like 'Think of those Ethiopian children as you tuck your own little ones up in bed at night' would not play well these days, nor deserve to.

Remember, too, that we are all surrounded by half-appreciated, half-digested facts that we relegate to the backs of our minds. Good fundraising copy can promote them to the front. And it does no harm to be as personal as possible.

'One in three of the population will suffer from cancer', or 'Ninety per cent of us will suffer from arthritis' are chastening and provocative sentences.

But 'One in three of us will suffer from cancer', or 'Your chances of escaping arthritis are just one in 10' are that much more challenging because the third person has been replaced by the second person and an objective fact has been given subjective power.

I was tempted to offer a couple of old shirts and some faded typewriter ribbons.

But there is nothing ethically wrong with pushing the point to its logical and most personal extreme.

One in three of your friends and family will suffer from cancer, or

Help us find a cure for arthritis before you get it.

No falsehoods are being deployed here. We have simply given the truth more power.

Ask for money and not support

I have already opined about the lazy overuse of the idiom of the 'supporter'. It is not how most donors see themselves – supporters are football fans not donors. But I await the debut of the dreaded 'stakeholders' in fundraising copy. Donors are already thus described within some charities and it can only be a matter of time before the first such salutation is sighted – *Dear Stakeholder.*

We don't seem to be comfortable with the simpler vocabulary of yesteryear. Hence our self-consciousness about the M word. Politicians have invented the word 'resources' to prevent them saying 'money' out loud and frightening the voters, for it sounds more mystical, less personally demanding. It goes without saying that charities have also begun to talk of resources. I have already received a mailing that talks of nothing else but the charity's need for 'more resources'. I was tempted to offer a couple of old shirts and some faded typewriter ribbons.

The word is money. Not support, or help, or contribution, or commitment (though each of these words has a place in a fundraiser's vocabulary). And it is extraordinary how seldom it is used.

The only exception surrounds those occasional situations where we are indeed asking for something other than money – participation in a sponsored event, a raffle, or a demonstration. But even here the M word could make an occasional appearance.

Remember Bob Geldof's appeal to the nation with BandAid in 1984? He did not say 'We need all the resources we can command.' He said 'Send us the f★★★★★ money.'

I rest my case.

Use 'I' and 'you'

Avoid the first person plural unless it is totally necessary – and it rarely is. This is a commonplace instruction for letter-writing on the obvious basis that letters should be seen to be completely individual communications between two human beings. But I am not sure that the I/you habit should be dropped from other parts of the communication. Why should an accompanying leaflet slip into a more formal and objective mode?

We are fortunate in English in using the pronoun 'you' in both singular and plural forms. But the second person plural can still make an accidental appearance in fundraising. 'Dear Friends' is a terrible way to start a letter. And do watch out for that corporate royal 'we'. 'We at the Royal Bank' is an appalling piece of pomp-speak. But 'we at Oxfam', or 'we in the environmental movement' are even worse for they suggest good causes adopting the verbal mores of corporations – not what most donors want to hear.

'Dear Friends' is a terrible way to start a letter.

Does it sound like someone talking? If not, why not?

This really is the summary of everything I have said so far. I have laboured the point for decades and embroidered the instruction by reading out random pieces of direct marketing or fundraising and trying to fit them into regular patterns of ordinary speech. A good audience will howl with laughter as they listen to the dislocation between the way we write and the way we speak.

Does it matter? I think it does, particularly in fundraising. We are now so bombarded with selling messages from every conceivable medium that we tune out those that are tiresome, or jaded, or boring, or just plain hysterical, either in content or in tone. We are aware of the verbal artifice and we react accordingly.

Fundraisers really have no excuse for communicating in other than acceptable human speech. Great issues do not need hysteria to be seen as great issues; the perception of need is not strengthened by the shrill language of the marketplace. We need passion, we need honesty and conviction, we need emotion, authority and urgency. We should not need verbal tricks.

There is one true test of whether your fundraising copy is effective. Read it out loud – to a colleague, your partner, or whoever. If they burst out laughing, you have written parody copy. If they fall silent, you have made an effect. If they threaten to blub, you have hit the jackpot.

All fundraising copy should sound like someone talking. Accept that and you will find that it is easier to write than the kind of inbred gibberish which so often scars an appeal.

Blah, blah, blah

Most fundraising appeals have too many words. The letter is usually longer than it needs to be and probably suffers from those ritualistic PSs. And we surround it with a leaflet or brochure as a further act of deference to the norm. Maybe we include a second letter by way of third-party endorsement. We certainly include that response device with its tick boxes, shopping list and other verbal rituals – and these days we will probably write copy on the back of it. Before we take stock, we have already used up perhaps 1,500 to 2,000 words to make our case. It is a tribute to the energy of the copywriter, but such verbosity should not be confused with good communication.

Yes, we write too many words. We spend endless time debating the nuances of those words. And we miss the only point that matters. It is sad but increasingly true – people do not read these words that we compile so assiduously. Indeed, they are bored witless at the very sight of them. The whole world is slipping into a post-verbal state where succinctness is seen as a greater virtue than coherence, the new world of the soundbite. Verbosity is suddenly a very old-fashioned practice restricted to charity mailings and, I guess, politicians.

Five deadly sins of direct mail copy

Welcome back to Curmudgeon's Corner. It helps me to list some of the dumb habits that copywriters in fundraising are falling into. So, it's cathartic. And, again, I think I sense the ghost of Orwell beaming at me as I write.

Polysyllables

Why on earth do we think that a long word is more impressive than a short one? They combine to form a language that is bureaucratic rather than human, corporate rather than personal. Fundraisers should mark the difference between these pairs of words

Approximately	About
Participate	Take part

Establish	Set up
Utilise	Use
Advise	Tell
Commence	Start
Complete	Fill in
Terminate	End

Think about it – why, in writing, do we ask people to *complete* a form when, across a desk, we would ask them to *fill in* the form? They seem so innocent, these more formal and posher words, but they always subtract a little meaning, reduce a little power.

Go looking for the equivalent long words that have clambered into your own vocabulary and which have learned to nestle there comfortably. Smother them.

Tautology

An increasing amount of words we use are redundant. And sometimes positively contradictory. We grow used to tautologies through sheer repetition. Thus,

A major nuclear disaster. So, what exactly is a minor nuclear disaster?

Said he had nothing further to add. The word 'further' is redundant.

Taking strike action. Workers used simply to strike.

First invented or discovered. How can you invent or discover something second?

Mutual agreement. Can an agreement be other than mutual?

Full and total support. A particularly sinister pairing of adjectives, this. For it has come to mean the precise opposite of what it says. A football manager who enjoys 'the full and total support' of his chairman is about to be fired. Likewise with politicians.

Died of a fatal dose of heroin. The cause of death is usually fatal!

I risk the accusation of pedantry in parading these examples. I guess that quite a few readers will have to look up the word tautology to see what I'm banging on about and, even then, they may have to think hard to see what's wrong with phrases like these. This makes my point for me. Tautology is a particularly pernicious thing if you cannot spot it.

Tautology is a particularly pernicious thing if you cannot spot it.

Jargon

The English language is currently in danger of breaking down into mutually discrete tribal patois, sub-languages that use a vocabulary rarely accessible to other tribes. This little book is written in tribal language – its excuse being that it is indeed produced for a very specialist audience.

But charities have their own jargon and they are in increasing danger of inflicting it on their donors.

The very word 'charity' seems slightly outmoded especially if you strut an international stage as an 'NGO' or 'development organisation'. About one donor in 10 might be able to decode these new verbal constructs. In North America, where the word 'charity' is pejorative they prefer the more modern but equally ambiguous 'nonprofit'.

And there is a touch of conspiracy about it as well. For the professional demand is to change the jargon constantly lest lay people begin to understand it or use it. There used to be 'under-developed countries'. Then they were 'developing countries', or maybe the Third World. In some quarters they are now The South and we The North (which leaves Australia deeply troubled).

Inevitably the jargon begins to infest the fundraising. What exactly is 'community development', or 'biodiversity', or 'skill sharing'? You can find words like these in most appeals these days. They come from the language of project workers and programme officers and it is often a lazy and opaque language, even within the field that invented it. To transfer it idly into fundraising is to risk complete reader stupefaction.

'Autoblag'

I invented this word years ago to describe the sort of copy you could write on mental autopilot. Your mind is switched off, you are going through the motions, yet somehow acceptable words and phrases seem to have issued from your word processor. The language of politics is now purely autoblag – you know not just what they are going to say but the very phrases with which they will say it.

I have begun to offer a deeply subversive homily about autoblag copy. It says, 'If your boss or client is comfortable with the copy, it is probably underachieving'. Sheer provocation, I know, but for a reason. It all comes back to Orwell's point about 'gumming together long lists of words'. You can get away with doing just that in a lot of professional situations. It is always wrong.

I have begun to offer a deeply subversive homily about autoblag copy.

A typical client brief these days will be longer than the copy it hopes to induce. But it offers only a ritual salaam to the process of thought. It may offer the mechanics of the appeal to be written but it will often tail off into a phrase like 'you know the sort of thing'. And, indeed, I do know the sort of thing. Indeed, I can produce copy absolutely guaranteed to arouse the heartening reaction 'yes, that's the sort of thing'. As a journeyman I can be satisfied with that reaction. As a writer I should be infinitely depressed. Words should be worth discussion, capable of improvement no matter how infuriating the debate. If they look right first time, if they are indeed 'the sort of thing', then both parties are probably presiding over mediocrity. It may work but it could have worked better.

Fundraising copy deserves better than comfort.

The handy cliché

I used to have a seminar slide that said 'Avoid clichés like the plague'. Not too many people got the joke.

Like tautology, clichés are pernicious – you need reminding that these easy constructs are indeed dull repetitions of words that have long since lost any power. Unfortunately we live in a society where much communication consists of stringing together cliché after cliché. People are forever 'moving the goalposts', or asking for a 'level playing field'. You cannot survive 15 minutes of the BBC Radio's *Today* programme without hearing 'at the end of the day'.

We are all guilty. For years I wrote copy for mail order catalogues, the sort that offered you apparently hi-tech gizmos – solar calculators that made the tea and changed colour with your mood swings (I exaggerate, but only a little). You rarely saw these products before writing about them, for they were usually being run up in Taiwan at the time. So you were forced back on a curious vocabulary of adjectives and adverbs that covered your graces. Everything was 'elegant', or 'beautiful', or 'distinctive'. If you had no idea what a product looked like, it could always be 'a conversation piece'. The joy of these desperate words was that you could move them around at will. Thus, something could be 'elegantly beautiful', or 'distinctively elegant'. *In extremis*, you would see the words 'a beautiful and elegant conversation piece that is truly distinctive'. Soon, clients began to look for these words in their copy. Another odd set of clichés had been invented. It is still in use.

Like much modern writing, it makes free use of the redundant adjective or adverb, the habit of bolting together an automatic epithet with a noun to make a cliché. Consider these, 'shocking facts', 'appalling truth', 'viciously attacked', 'prompt action', 'chilling accounts', 'savagely beaten', 'cruelly neglected', 'isolated case', 'appropriate action', 'urgent need'. It is as if each of these nouns had come pre-wrapped with a familiar adjective. And I found all of these bolt-on clichés in one short letter from a child-care organisation. Each of the powerful truths it told could have been reported more powerfully if more attention had been given to alternative words or alternative means of expression. It is autoblag again.

Words should be worth discussion, capable of improvement no matter how infuriating the debate.

Why does every appeal for a committed giving scheme insist on preceding '£2 a week' or '£3 a week' (a cliché in itself, of course) with the word 'just' or 'only'?

Why does everyone who reads out a phone number for a radio charity appeal have to repeat it with the word 'that's' before the repetition? Why does a certain kind of radio commercial always end with the message 'we're waiting by the phones'?

It is because charities assume that there is a verbal model for every kind of communication, one from which they depart at their peril. It is yet another example of clinging desperately to formulae, like shipwrecked mariners clinging to the wreckage in the belief that it is a life raft.

Each of the powerful truths it told could have been reported more powerfully if more attention had been given to alternative words or alternative means of expression.

Five under-used virtues – for occasional use only

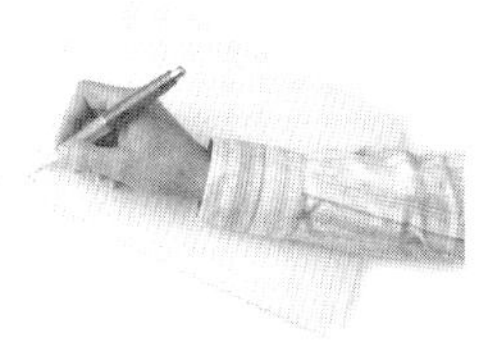

Occasionally you can step way outside the copywriting manual and do something without precedent. Well, not totally without precedent of course for nothing is ever really new. But occasionally a set of circumstances takes shape that enables you to write in a totally different mode or style and still be successful. The very unexpectedness of your message helps, of course, and you cannot by definition make a habit of it. But it does help underline the point that any little spark of verbal life will attract better readership and therefore better response.

Candour

Talk to some fundraisers and you can be forgiven for imagining that the prime purpose of their charities is to send fundraising appeals. Most of them would be well advised to mail less often and more thoughtfully but the fundraising machine is not easily thrust into idle. To suggest that the whole appeals mailing programme could be abolished is to colour yourself in as mad, bad and dangerous to know. Heavens, if there were no appeals mailing programme, there would be no need for a Direct Marketing Manager, the data wallahs and the several creative teams involved. Where would it all end?

Only occasionally do you get the chance to pursue such heresy. In the early 1990s Charter 88 was a powerful lobbying group advocating constitutional change in the UK. It got famous quickly and soon acquired 60,000 supporters who, inevitably, were regularly asked for money to support the campaign's work.

There was a traditional four-appeals-a-year programme aimed at conjuring an average of £25 a year from each supporter (there was no membership subscription). It worked but only in the face of mass groaning from Charter 88 enthusiasts. They were, after all, recruited exclusively from liberal broadsheets. They were lawyers and teachers and doctors. They probably had two and half degrees each. And there we were, sending them begging letters every three months

As I said, it worked. We always made budget. But the situation demanded a little mischief-making. If we were mailing four times a year in the expectation of £25 per name, why not ask them for the £25 in the first place and spare a few trees? It was time for candour.

And please send us a contribution to help our work. It always pains us when we write to you that we have to conclude our reporting back with that time-honoured phrase about needing more money. We know full well that you will receive many such letters that ask you for financial support. And we know full well that it must be tiresome in the extreme.

Can we suggest a way to spare both of us this regular embarrassment? If you can send us a donation of £25 or more either by cheque or standing order in response to this letter, we promise not to ask you again for money during 1991. We will continue to keep you updated with information about the campaign and we may even ask you to do other things to help us. But we will spare you the regular begging. We may be the first cause group to talk to its supporters with this kind of honest maturity, but we're not going to be ashamed of that. We need the money badly but we hate the mendicant mode.

This simple mailing achieved Charter 88's best ever response in its early days. Was it because all their supporters were highly intelligent or worldly? Was it because the language was refreshingly unorthodox? Was it because it made an offer that few would refuse? I shall never really know but will always feel privileged to have had a client prepared to licence such adventure. And, indeed, to have sanctioned a phrase like 'the mendicant mode'.

Inevitably this became quite a famous case history, reported in books, presented on platforms. But I never heard of anyone trying it again, or of developing further the concept of allowing the supporters to buy themselves out of a mailing programme. Perhaps candour is just too dangerous a commodity for charities.

Rhetoric

Why are we so afraid of eloquent or elegant writing? We deceive ourselves by presuming that we must always express ourselves in the same lowest-common-denominator prose that disfigures so much of our contemporary culture. The current appeal of Jane Austen adaptations and the new generation of Shakespeare films may lie to some extent in our love of pageant and beautiful costumes; for myself, I choose to believe that it reflects our need to be subjected, at least occasionally, to the thrill of fine language. I would advise any contemporary politician to suspend the dismal litany of soundbites and start developing the verbal ambition of a Lincoln or a Churchill. Votes, I suspect, would follow such ambition.

Why are we so afraid of eloquent or elegant writing?

For words can thrill and words can motivate. Yet this rhetorical power is rarely to be seen in fundraising communication. When it does appear, your attention is grabbed. It isn't an appeal letter any more – it's a poem, a novel, a speech. This is how a letter from Greenpeace Canada started a few years back.

Great towering trees straining for the sky.

Their lush verdant canopies covering a moist and humid world playing host to a super abundance of life. Jaguars, toucans, orang-utans, pythons, tigers and giant sloths. In all, five million species of animals, birds, fish, reptiles, insects and plants. Fifty per cent of all living things. Such is the wonder of the rain forest.

The incessant whine of the chain saw and the deafening roar of the bulldozer threatens this cornucopia of life. Every minute of every hour of every day 100 acres of irreplaceable rain forest are destroyed or seriously damaged.

It's easy to pick holes in these paragraphs for they smack just a little of a fifth form essay. But it is the general effect that matters. Someone has been trying for poetry, someone has tried to describe a familiar issue with a certain passionate eloquence. You will read further into this letter because it tries so hard at the beginning to catch you at your thoughtful best.

Sometimes it pays to suspend self-consciousness and see how our message might sound if it were pitched at a verbally more ambitious level. Rhetoric can work. Not all the time, admittedly, but on occasion. It is another underused virtue.

Brevity

I made the point earlier that fundraisers use too many words in print. We seem more comfortable with a strange verbosity, as if our first duty is to tick off the 11 items in the written brief rather than produce a compelling message.

Consider this one-piece mailing from the Canadian Red Cross. Above this letter is the response device/address carrier. The reverse gives you basic statistics about the Red Cross in Ontario. And that's it!

Dear Friend,

DISASTER! It can strike anywhere, anytime.

And, when it does, the Red Cross Society knows how to help.

In a matter of moments – perhaps in the time it takes you to read this paragraph – disaster could be striking somewhere, even affecting the life of someone you know.

Please make sure the Red Cross is there ready to help. I urge you to take a moment now to write a generous cheque. A donation of $25 or more will qualify you as a Sustaining Member of the Society.

Thank you
Sincerely

John R Finley

President, Ontario Division.

You could argue that such brevity is presumptuous, that the success of the letter (and like the Greenpeace one, it is a long-standing control pack) relies on the universal understanding of the Red Cross and its work. But I am still left wondering how much more successful we might be if we gave the reader less to read.

Why not explore the thesis? Test a standard two-page letter against a one-page letter. Omit the leaflet. Cut everything to the bone. I have an awful feeling that your tests will show little variance of response. And you will, of course, have spent a little less on the process.

Rewriting everything

Every now and again it makes sense to move the furniture around at home. The room looks totally different. You realise that the wing of an armchair has been blocking the television. You find things under cushions. You expose the awfulness of that painting you were given 10 years back. You always intended to do something about the room and you always half knew what was wrong with it.

The same applies to fundraising copy. We get used to it, too lazy to change things. In particular, we get used to those parts of the copy that seem never quite to need change – the semi-statutory paragraphs with which every piece of fundraising communication is inevitably studded. In the UK, this includes deathless phrases about the Data Protection Act, the ritual incantations about GiftAid and that time-honoured sentence about not needing a stamp but how the charity saves money if you use one (vintage 1971, just for the record). All these things could be rewritten. And all these things *should* be rewritten on the simple basis that more people would then read them and react to them. Take that ugly apology we have sometimes to make when we are worried about mis-addressing or picking up an existing donor with a widespread cold appeal. Why not use plain English? Why not make it sound fresh and genuine? Why not turn it into a selling point?

Amnesty Canada did all these things. This copy sits on the back of the outer envelope in an acquisition pack.

Sometimes mistakes happen. You may receive more than one copy of the same letter from Amnesty, or you may already be a donor. We try hard to stop this happening, but sometimes the computer records contain two slightly different variations of your name and address. You can help us. If you receive a package with a mailing label that has an error in your name and/or address, please correct it and send it back to us with your donation.

> For the personal anecdote will always outgun any global statistics about trade, or any sophisticated argument about development theory.

If you receive more than one package, we suggest that you pass the extra one on to someone who is concerned about human rights violations.

Okay, the last bit is a tad presumptive. But the rest of it sounds totally honest, straightforward and, indeed, businesslike. It shows how much more you can achieve when you continue to challenge every phrase you ever write, be it ever so humble. I just hope that Amnesty have changed the wording since. The point about moving the furniture around is that you are never quite going to be satisfied. Nor should you be.

The first person imperative

Yes, the best fundraising letters are written on a straight I/you basis. And the very best fundraising letters are written, or purport to be written, by people working in the frontline of need rather than their intermediaries. You cannot get more powerful than this Oxfam letter, written in1987 by Marcus Thompson, one of their senior field officers at the time.

Dear Supporter,

Doesn't it upset you to walk among people who have lost everything? Doesn't it distress you to see small children dying in their mothers' arms?

I am often asked these questions when I return from a disaster zone. Quite frankly, it does and it doesn't...

It doesn't because I'm busy when I'm visiting the scene of a disaster. I don't feel the helplessness you feel in front of your TV set. Just the opposite, I have the privilege of being able to do something to ease the suffering.

But of course it hurts when someone you've got to know dies.

In the civil war in Uganda I was visiting camps for people fleeing the fighting. We picked up a very sick mother and her starving children to take them to hospital in Kampala. In the crowded jeep a little boy of five or six sat on my lap. We smiled at each other as the jeep bounced along the rough dirt road. He died before we reached the hospital.

That evening I just dissolved into tears. I have a child about the same age.

This cannot possibly be anything but an honest man talking. You have just read it – and I think you were moved. You may just be flicking away tears yourself.

You never seem to see letters like this any more. Perhaps charities regard themselves as demeaned by language so emotional. Perhaps they feel that the Marcus Thompsons on their payroll are not the most correct of advocates. They should realise that the ability to send a message like this is privilege indeed. For the personal anecdote will always outgun any global statistics about trade, or any sophisticated argument about development theory.

But, no, you cannot make a habit of formatting your appeals in this first person documentary style. Like anything else, it would get tiresome and predictable and would be dismissed accordingly. It is a powerful tool, available to just about any charity or cause. It should be used sparingly. It will always be used successfully.

Envoi

I hope this slimmest of volumes may help you make more money. But I also hope that it gets you into the habit of thinking about every part of the job of fundraising. It gets harder every year, that job. So we are simply going to have to get better at it.

Remember: we are not machine-minders but makers of a better world. Never lose sight of the distinction between the two.

GS

A promise from The White Lion Press

Enjoy the best books on fundraising.

Books by The White Lion Press will repay your investment many times over – and you'll enjoy reading them too. But if your purchase is damaged in any way, or if you feel any of our products do not live up to your expectations simply return them to us and we will issue you with a full refund, including any reasonable associated costs. We'll ask you to tell us why, so we can put right anything that might be wrong, but we won't quibble. Unfortunately we can only offer this if you bought the book directly from us, but even if you didn't, please let us know your problem and we'll do all we can to ensure your supplier matches our commitment to you. After all, you are our ultimate customer.

This guarantee applies to any books or videos you may purchase from us. We further promise to handle your orders with speed, efficiency and impressive politeness.

If you wish to order further titles, please detach or photocopy the order form at the back of the book and either send it to us by fax or post. You can also order by e-mailing orders@whitelionpress.com.

If you have any query at all regarding any books published by The White Lion Press please telephone Marie Burnett on +33 (0)2 97 39 52 63, or by fax on +33 (0)2 97 39 57 69, or by email at mail@whitelionpress.com.

Tiny Essentials of Fundraising

by Neil Sloggie
Softback, 57 pp. ISBN 0-9518971-5-2

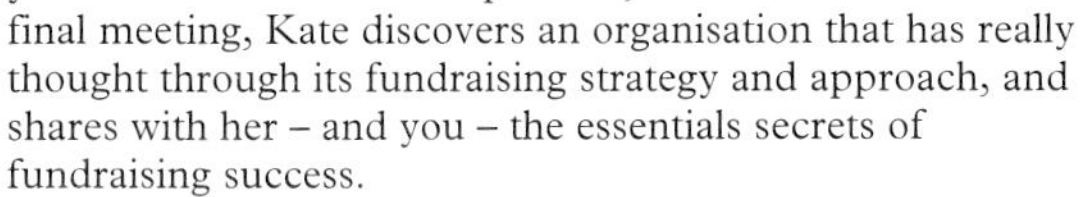

All you really need to know about fundraising, in one tiny book.

Join Kate, an inquisitive and ambitious new recruit to the fundraising profession, as she sets out to uncover what really matters in her chosen career by visiting and asking three seasoned practitioners. Like Kate you'll see as much to avoid as to emulate in the first two encounters but you'll be reassured and inspired as, in her final meeting, Kate discovers an organisation that has really thought through its fundraising strategy and approach, and shares with her – and you – the essentials secrets of fundraising success.

'A simple and truthful reminder of what's at the heart of effective fundraising. How I wish someone had given me this book when I was starting out all those years ago!'
Jan Chisholm, Fundraising Manager, Greenpeace, Australia.

'I was given a copy of the 'Tiny' book in Australia and was so enamoured of the clear message it conveys that I ordered a special edition to give to more than 1,500 fundraisers and all 700 Blackbaud employees. Their reactions have been universally positive. *Tiny Essentials of Fundraising* is one of those books that make us truly envious of the author for executing such a brilliant piece of writing...'
Robert Sywolski, chief executive, Blackbaud Inc, USA.

'Its a smart idea, well-executed – how fabulous to have a bite-sized book that sums up what makes for successful fundraising in such an accessible way to both native and non-native English speakers.

'Great stuff. Thanks Neil for what must be the shortest, simplest and yet very salient contribution to the world's literature on fundraising.'
Julie Weston, UNHCR, Switzerland.

Relationship Fundraising: A Donor-based Approach to the Business of Raising Money (second edition)

By Ken Burnett
Published by Jossey-Bass Inc in association with The White Lion Press Limited.
Hardback, 384 pp. ISBN 0-7879-6089-6

Ken Burnett has completely revised and updated his classic book *Relationship Fundraising*. Filled with illustrative case examples, donor profiles, and more than 200 action points, this ground-breaking book shows fundraisers how to

- Implement creative approaches to relationship-building fundraising
- Avoid common fundraising errors and pitfalls
- Apply the vital ingredients for fundraising success
- Build good relationships with donors through marketing
- Achieve a greater understanding of donors
- Communicate effectively with donors – using direct mail, the press, television, the telephone, face-to-face contact, and more
- Prepare for the challenges of twenty-first century fundraising.

'Not since Harold Seymour's classic, *Designs for Fund Raising*, has a book of this magnitude come along.

'Ken Burnett's updated and expanded work, *Relationship Fundraising*, just may be the book to which fundraising professionals turn for the next several decades.

'It is as brilliant as it is heartfelt, as simple as it is eloquent.'
Jerry Cianciolo, *The Compleat Professional's Library, Contributions Magazine*, USA.

'Ken Burnett's observations, insights and practical tips for building and sustaining relationships are superb. Highly readable, this book is a solid mix of sound theory and pragmatic application.'
Kay Sprinkel Grace, author, *Beyond Fund Raising*; co-author *High Impact Philanthropy*, USA.

'This is the book that sets the agenda for fundraising communications in the twenty-first century. Engaging, inspiring, and thought-provoking, *Relationshp Fundraising* is based on the unique 25-year experience of one of the world's most respected fundraisers.'

Bernard Ross, director, The Management Centre, UK; co-author, *Breakthrough Thinking for Nonproft Organizations.*

Friends for Life: Relationship Fundraising in Practice

By Ken Burnett
Hardback, 599 pp. ISBN 0-9518971-2-8

Amid the widespread acclaim that greeted the 1992 publication of Ken Burnett's *Relationship Fundraising* was one persistent qualified comment. Essentially the question was 'relationship fundraising sounds very attractive, but will it help us raise more money?'

In this accessible and entertaining sequel Ken Burnett describes how relationship fundraising is working in a wide variety of organisations in the USA, Canada and the United Kingdom. Their stories provide the answer: a loud and clear 'yes!'

But the ideas and experiences described in this book will do much more than just help fundraisers raise more money. It will show them how to develop and maintain strong, healthy, mutually beneficial relationships with their donors; relationships that will enable them to make friends for life.

The sequel to *Relationship Fundraising* first appeared in 1996, to international acclaim.

'I'm an enthusiastic fan of Ken Burnett's approach to building friends for life. His new book builds on the practical, common-sense approach to donor development he is famous for advocating.

'Great examples, an easy read – I highly recommend *Friends for Life: Relationship Fundraising in Practice.*'

Dr Judith E Nichols, CFRE, author and consultant, USA.

'*Friends for Life* is a witty, readable tour of donor-think from both sides of the Atlantic and brings together a unique collection of experiences and anecdotes from many world-class fundraisers. *Relationship Fundraising* is already a classic throughout the world and

this sequel is sure to have a similar impact.'
Jennie Thompson, consultant and co-founder of Craver, Mathews, Smith and Company, USA.

'The Botton Village case history is riveting. Its lessons have a relevance beyond fundraising. This is what direct marketing should always be, but so seldom is.'
Graeme McCorkell, author and consultant, UK.

Asking Properly: The Art of Creative Fundraising

By George Smith
Hardback, 220 pp. ISBN 0-9518971-1-X

You will never read a book quite like this. George Smith tears open the conventional wisdom of fundraising creativity and so changes the rules for an entire trade. This book is irreverent, funny, savagely critical and genuinely inspiring, often on the same page.

Asking Properly is almost certainly the most authoritative book ever written about the creative aspects of fundraising. It is likely to remain a key text for years to come.

The author offers a profound analysis of donor motivation and is critical of the extent to which charities take their supporters for granted. But this book is no mere commentary on current practice – it offers a comprehensive checklist on how to optimise the creative presentation of the fundraising message. How to write, design, use direct mail, press advertising, broadcast media and the telephone, how to think in terms of fundraising products…the whole gallery of creativity and media is surveyed and assessed, with hundreds of examples of fundraising campaigns from around the world illustrating the need to 'ask properly'.

The book will prove invaluable to anyone involved in the fundraising process. It is provocative, entertaining and, above all, highly instructive. Read it, apply its lessons and it must enable you to raise more money.

'This book will become a classic. It's not just inspirational and a great read, there's a practical benefit on every page. When you apply George Smith's secrets you can hardly fail to improve your fundraising.'

Harvey McKinnon, president, Harvey McKinnon & Associates, Canada.

'It's typically George Smith: wise, uncompromising, devastatingly critical of poor fundraising, brilliantly illustrative of what is good, full of ideas, funny, marvellously written – and exceptionally good value. In short, *Asking Properly* is one of those very few books you will keep for life.'

Pierre-Bernard Le Bas, head of fundraising, UNHCR, Switzerland.

Friends for Life video series

A series of half hour videos from the Friends for Life sessions featuring Ken Burnett in Vancouver, Canada in July 1996. Filmed by Canada's Knowledge Network and produced jointly by Harvey McKinnon & Associates and The White Lion Press.

Video One

- The challenge of relationship fundraising
- How to introduce world-class donor service
- Getting ahead of your competition

Video Two

- Botton Village: the classic case history of superb relationship fundraising
- How you can profit from your donor's will
- Four highly successful fundraising programmes

Cost £35.00 for both videos, individually £20.00 each plus postage and packing.

Please return to The White Lion Press Limited,
Kermarquer, 56310 Melrand, France.

Telephone: +33 (0)2 97 39 52 63. Fax: +33 (0)2 97 39 57 59.
Email: orders@whitelionpress.com

Please send me the following titles

No of copies	Title	Price*£	P &P**£	Total £
______	Tiny Essentials of Fundraising	£7.95	______	______
______	Tiny Essentials of Writing for Fundraising	£7.95	______	______
______	Relationship Fundraising	£19.00	______	______
______	Relationship Fundraising second edition	£25.50	______	______
______	Friends for Life	£21.00	______	______
______	Asking Properly	£24.00	______	______
______	Video one	£20.00	______	______
______	Video two	£20.00	______	______
______	Both videos	£35.00	______	______

* With the exceptions of the second edition of *Relationship Fundraising* and both 'Tinys', if you order any two titles from this list you will be entitled to a 10 per cent discount on the retail price of each book. Orders of three copies or more will entitle you to a 20 per cent discount. (NB these offers only apply to orders placed directly with the publisher.) For bulk orders on *Relationship Fundraising*, second edition and *Tiny Essentials of Fundraising* please contact orders@whitelionpress.com.

** For postage and packing to European destinations please add £3.55 for either edition of *Relationship Fundraising*. For all other countries add £4.60 per copy. For postage and packing for *Friends for Life* and *Asking Properly* to European destinations, please add £4.95 and £7.75 to all other countries. Postage and packing to a European address for either 'Tiny' is £1.87 and £2.23 to all other countries. Postage and packing for video 1 or 2 is £2.15 (Europe), £2.73 to all other countries. For both videos please add £3.55 (Europe) or £4.60 to all other countries.

I enclose a cheque for £______ payable to The White Lion Press Limited.

Please bill my organisation at the address below.

Please debit my Visa/AmEx/Mastercard. Number:

Signature ____________________ Expiry date __________

Your name ______________________________

Organisation ______________________________

Your position ______________________________

Address ______________________________

____

____

____________________ Postcode __________

Telephone ______________________________

Fax ______________________________

Email ______________________________